THIS BOOK BELONGS TO...

Name:	Age:

Favourite player:

2022-2023

My Predictions...	Actual...
The Swans' final position:	
The Swans' top scorer:	
Sky Bet Championship winners:	
Sky Bet Championship top scorer:	
FA Cup winners:	
EFL Cup winners:	

Contributors: Peter Rogers

A TWOCAN PUBLICATION

ISBN: 978-1-914588-70-9

£10

PICTURE CREDITS: Action Images, Alamy, Athena Picture Agency, Natalie Davis, Press Association, Swansea City AFC.

TOGETHER
EFL

CONTENTS

GOAL OF THE SEASON

The second it was scored, it was going to take some beating. While Michael Obafemi takes the plaudits for being there to put the ball in the net, it was the way the Swans forwards linked up to seamlessly carve rivals Cardiff City apart which ensured the goal stood out to the voting fans.

The goal was the first of four for the Swans who created history with a comprehensive 4-0 victory at the Cardiff City Stadium, which backed up a 3-0 win earlier in the season at home. The two results meant they achieved the first South Wales league derby double and completed it in some style.

Each of the goals were spectacular in their own way, but the play between attacking trio Jamie Paterson, Joel Piroe and Michael Obafemi to create the 2022-23 goal of the season was Russell Martin's Swansea City at their fluid best.

MICHAEL OBAFEMI

It was just six minutes into the game when Matt Grimes played the ball into the feet of Paterson, he laid it off to Piroe, who played into the feet of Obafemi. The striker played it first time around the corner to Paterson who was already on the move and the winger had the simplest of squared balls back to Obafemi - unmarked in the six yard box - to tap in past the scrambling keeper.

Swansea
University
Prifysgol
Abertawe

NUMBER OF SEASONS WITH THE SWANS:

2

SWANS LEAGUE APPEARANCES:

69

SWANS LEAGUE GOALS:

11

LEGEND

ADRIAN FORBES

SWANS ACHIEVEMENTS:

League Two promotion winners 2004-05

Football League Trophy winners 2005-06

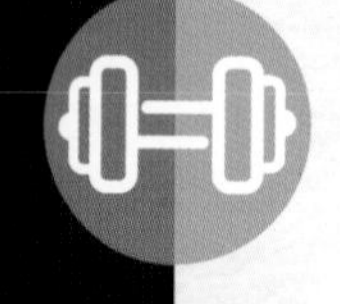

MAJOR STRENGTH:

Blistering pace and a great eye for goal

INTERNATIONAL ACTION:

A former England U18 player, he didn't play any international football with Swansea

FINEST HOUR:

Adrian Forbes famously scored the club's last league goal at the Vetch in 2005

Top quality attacking midfielders Adrian Forbes and Scott Sinclair were two of the most exciting wide-men to pull on the famous white Swansea City shirt and both made a big impression during their respective careers at the club.

Forbes and Sinclair were clear match winners on their day and blessed with the skill, pace and talent to turn games in the Swans' favour. With the ability to score goals and create chances for teammates, these two former Swansea City stars were both real crowd favourites at the Vetch and the Swansea.com Stadium. Both players starred for Swansea City in exciting and successful times for the club - but who was the best? That's for you to decide and here are a few facts and figures from their time in Swansea colours to help you reach your conclusion...

It's a tough call...!

LEGEND

SCOTT SINCLAIR

NUMBER OF SEASONS WITH THE SWANS:

3

SWANS LEAGUE APPEARANCES:

82

SWANS LEAGUE GOALS:

28

SWANS ACHIEVEMENTS:

Championship Play-Off winners 2010-11

MAJOR STRENGTH:

Great ability to glide past defenders and a cool finisher in and around the penalty area

INTERNATIONAL ACTION:

Scott played for England U21s and the Great Britain Olympic team while he was a Swansea player

FINEST HOUR:

Sinclair was the Swans' hat-trick hero in the 2010-11 Play-Off victory over Reading as the club secured Premier League status

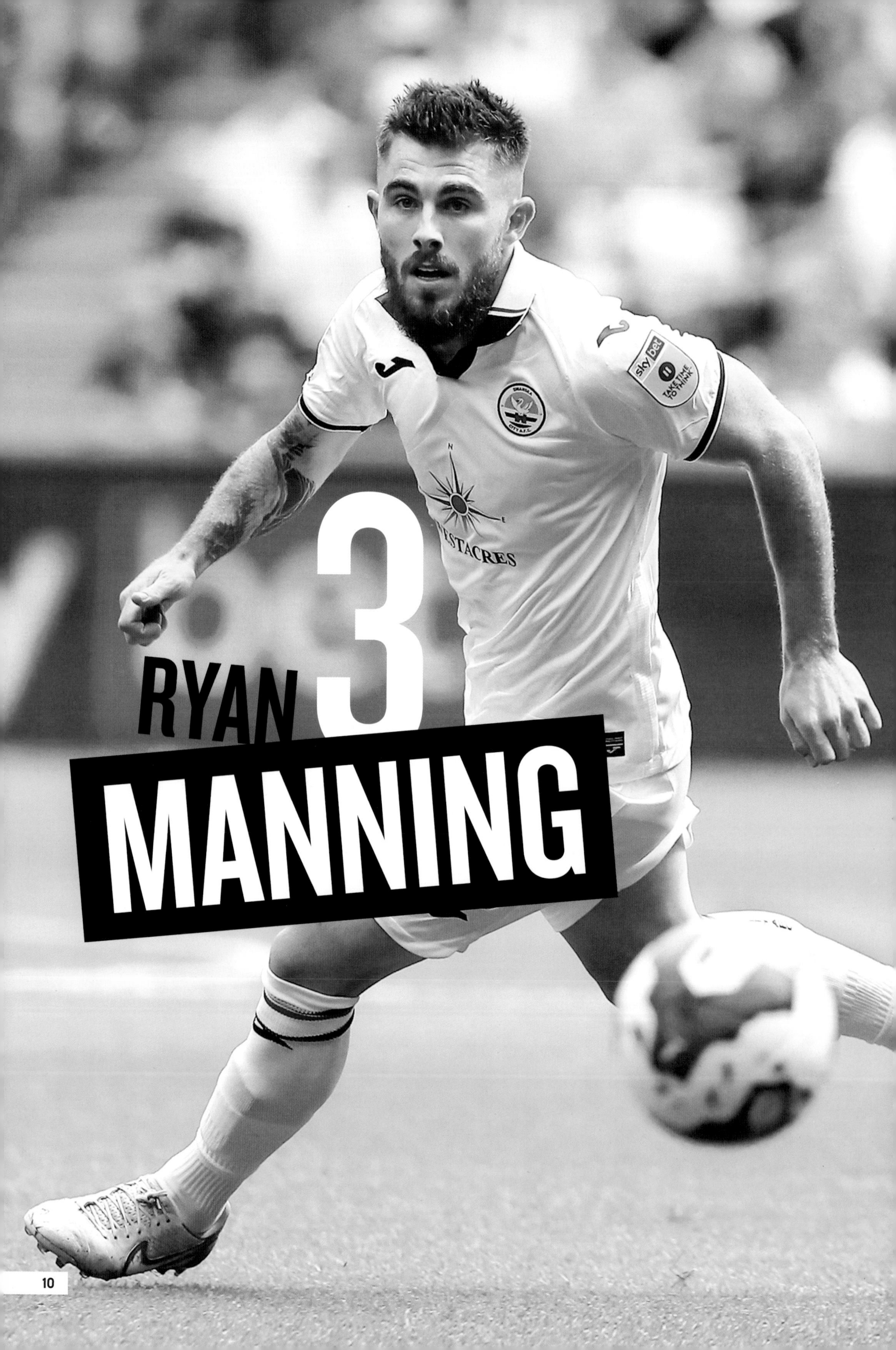
RYAN
3
MANNING

Defending is not just about stopping the attackers and clearing your lines. Making the best of possession you have just won is vital - although the danger has to be cleared, it is important for your team to keep hold of the ball.

SOCCER SKILLS

LONG PASSES

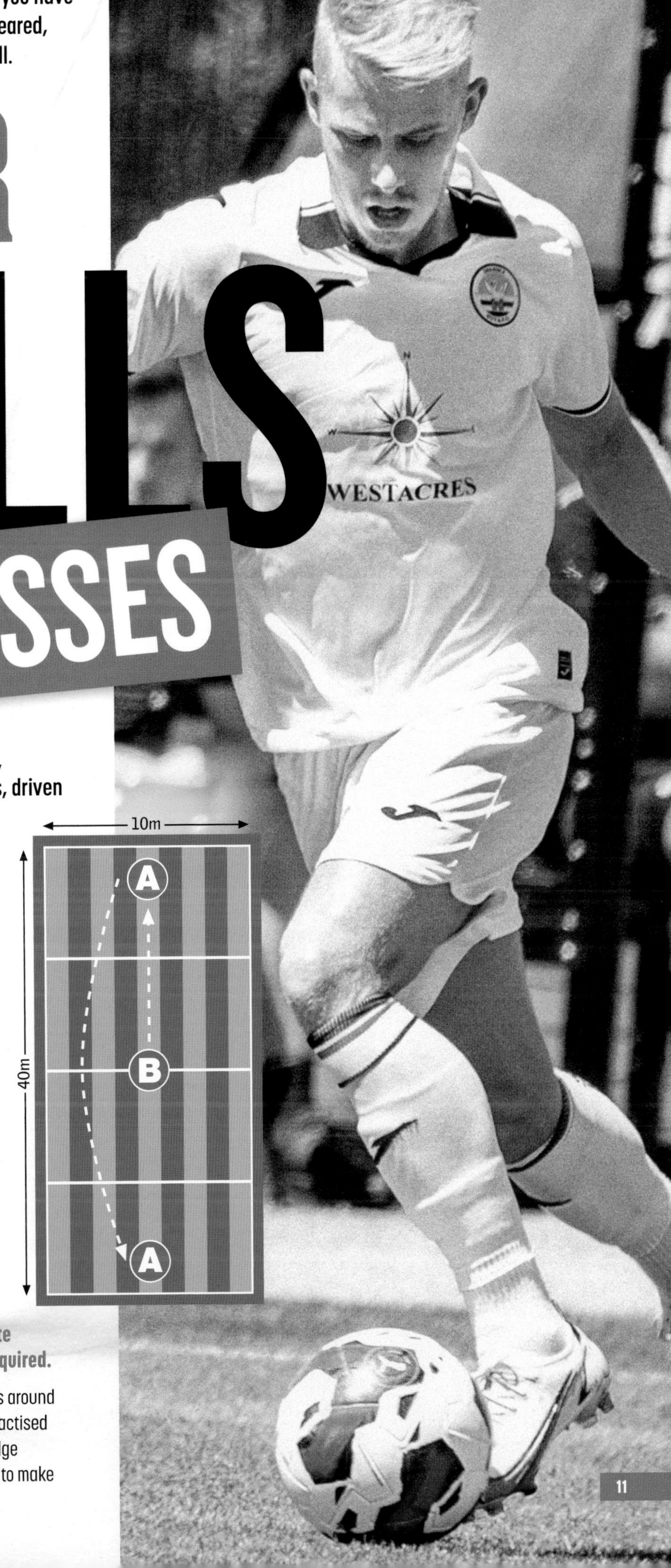

When passing your way out of defence, and short, side-foot passes are not possible, the longer pass, driven over the heads of midfield players, can be used.

EXERCISE

In an area 40m x 10m, A1 and A2 try to pass accurately to each other, with a defender B, in the middle between them. Player B must attempt to stop the pass if possible, and A1 and A2, must keep the ball within the area of the grids.

After each successful long pass, the end player will exchange a shorter pass with B before passing long again, thus keeping the exercise realistic and also keeping the defender in the middle involved. The player in the middle should be changed every few minutes, and a 'count' of successful passes made for each player.

KEY FACTORS

1 Approach at an angle.
2 Non kicking foot placed next to the ball.
3 Eye on the ball.
4 Strike underneath the ball & follow through.

Practice is the key to striking a consistently accurate long pass and to developing the timing and power required.

The same end result could be achieved by bending the pass around the defender instead of over him, and this pass could be practised in the same exercise, by striking the football on its outer edge (instead of underneath) which will impart the spin required to make the ball 'bend' around the defender - not an easy skill!

CHAMPIONSHIP 2022-2023

SQUAD

1 ANDY FISHER

GOALKEEPER DOB: 12/02/1998 COUNTRY: ENGLAND

The Blackburn Rovers academy product signed professional terms at Ewood Park in 2016 making four appearances.

After a loan spell at MK Dons he was signed permanently at the club in 2020. He made the switch to Swans in January 2022 making 19 appearances and keeping five clean sheets in his first six-months at SA1.

3 RYAN MANNING

DEFENDER DOB: 14/06/1996 COUNTRY: ROI

The Ireland international made the move to south Wales from Queens Park Rangers in 2020.

He'd spent five years in London following his move from League of Ireland side Galway United at the age of 19. He is a versatile player and can operate in midfield, at left-back and in a back three.

4 JAY FULTON

MIDFIELDER DOB: 01/04/1994 COUNTRY: SCOTLAND

The long-serving midfielder has been at Swansea for eight years and is one of just two players still at the club to have represented the Swans in the top flight.

During the 2015-16 season, he was part of the team to beat both Arsenal and Liverpool. In total, he has made more than 170 appearances for the Swans.

CHAMPIONSHIP 2022-2023 SQUAD

5 BEN CABANGO

DEFENDER DOB: 30/05/2000 COUNTRY: WALES

Academy product and Wales international Ben Cabango slowly made his way through the ranks before becoming a first-team regular during the 2021-22 season.

He made 100 senior Swans appearances before his 22 birthday and scored a memorable goal against Cardiff City in April 2022.

6 HARRY DARLING

DEFENDER DOB: 08/08/1999 COUNTRY: ENGLAND

The former Cambridge United and MK Dons man joined Swansea City in the summer of 2022.

The 23-year-old made a impactful debut scoring from 25-yards to rescue a point against Rotherham United. He's made a bit of a name for himself as a goal-scorer hitting double figures during the 2021-22 campaign.

7 JOE ALLEN

MIDFIELDER DOB: 14/03/1990 COUNTRY: WALES

The homecoming story of the summer, Allen returned to the club where it all started for him after a decade away.

He joined Swans at the age of 9 and made more than 150 senior appearances in club colours before following manager Brendan Rodgers to Liverpool. He returned as a free agent after leaving Stoke City. He is one of Wales' most influential players in recent history earning more than 70 international caps.

CHAMPIONSHIP 2022-2023 SQUAD

8 MATT GRIMES

MIDFIELDER DOB: 15/07/1995 COUNTRY: ENGLAND

The Exeter academy product joined Swans in 2015. After a difficult few years, he found his footing under Graham Potter and became instrumental that season making 50 appearances.

His calm head and range of passing is key to the Swans style of play. He was named captain ahead of the 2019-20 season.

9 MICHAEL OBAFEMI

ATTACKER DOB: 06/07/2000 COUNTRY: ROI

Charismatic front man Michael Obafemi had a slow start to life in SA1 after joining from Southampton in August 2021.

He hit his stride around February though and went on to score eleven goals in 18 games thanks in part to a burgeoning partnership with Joel Piroe.

10 OLIVIER NTCHAM

MIDFIELDER DOB: 09/02/1996 COUNTRY: CAMEROON

The French-born Cameroonian International joined Swans from Celtic in September 2021 and became something of an impact player mostly being utilised off the bench.

He has had a varied career first arriving in the UK when he signed a five-year deal at Premier League champions Manchester City. Following a loan to Genoa, he made the move to Scotland and then south Wales.

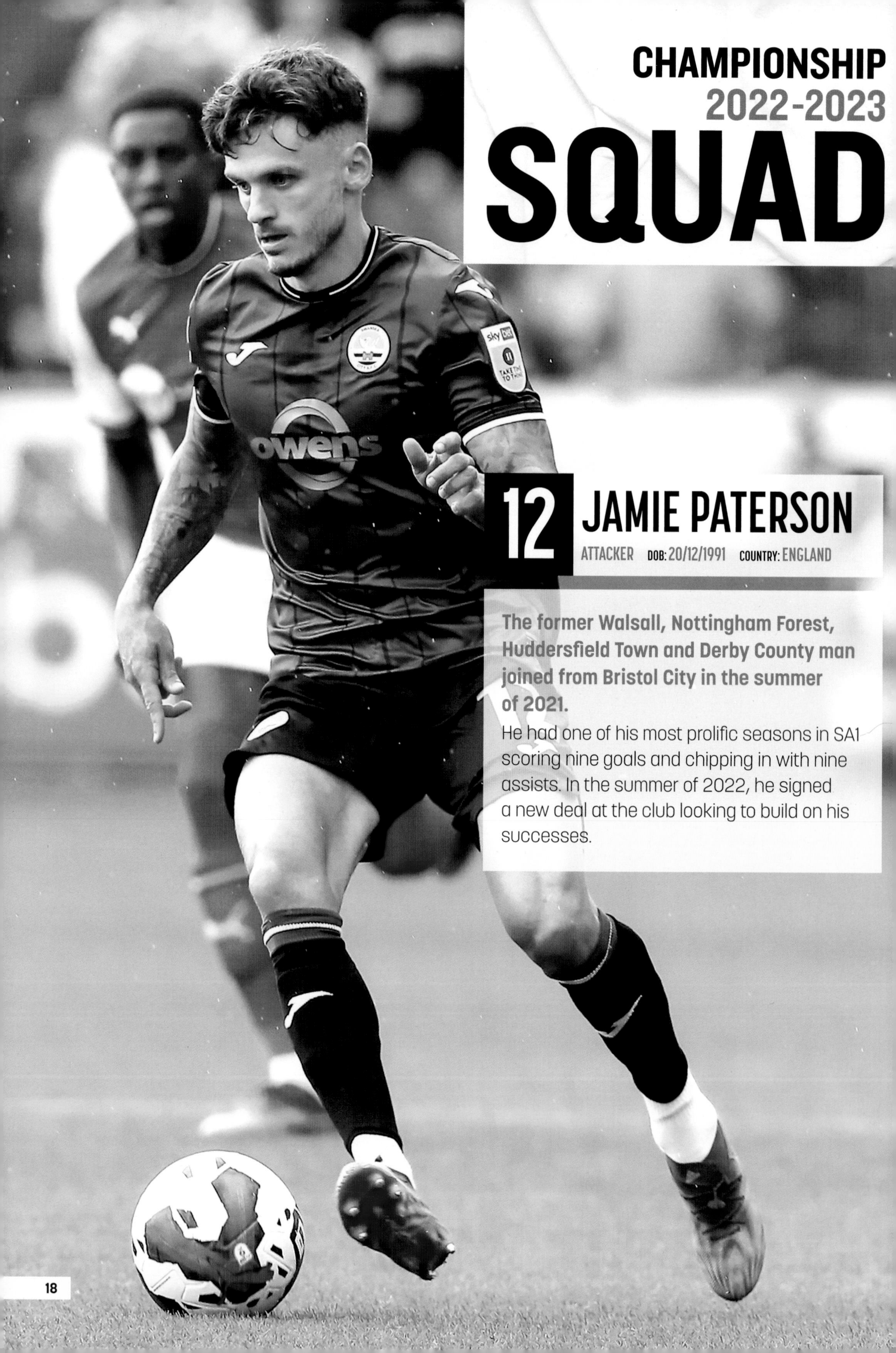

CHAMPIONSHIP 2022-2023 SQUAD

12 JAMIE PATERSON

ATTACKER DOB: 20/12/1991 COUNTRY: ENGLAND

The former Walsall, Nottingham Forest, Huddersfield Town and Derby County man joined from Bristol City in the summer of 2021.

He had one of his most prolific seasons in SA1 scoring nine goals and chipping in with nine assists. In the summer of 2022, he signed a new deal at the club looking to build on his successes.

13 STEVEN BENDA

GOALKEEPER DOB: 01/10/1998 COUNTRY: GERMANY

German shot-stopper Steven Benda joined Swans academy from TSV 1860 München as an 18-year-old and has made six senior appearances.

He has also had loan spells at Swindon Town and Peterborough United.

15 NATHANAEL OGBETA

DEFENDER DOB: 28/04/2001 COUNTRY: ENGLAND

The speedy wing-back's time at Swans so far has been hampered by injury.

Signing on deadline day from Shrewsbury Town in January 2021, he was side-lined for several months finally making his debut off the bench in March.

16 BRANDON COOPER

DEFENDER DOB: 14/01/2000 COUNTRY: WALES

Bridgend-born defender Brandon Cooper joined Swans academy aged six years old and worked his way through the ranks making his senior debut against Crystal Palace in the EFL Cup in August 2018.

He went on to make a further ten appearances in Swans colours between loan spells at Yeovil Town, Newport County and Swindon Town.

17 JOEL PIROE

ATTACKER DOB: 02/08/1999 COUNTRY: NETHERLANDS

Signed from PSV Eindhoven in the summer of 2021, the Dutchman very much 'started as he meant to go on' opening his Swans account with a goal on his debut.

He went on to score a total 24 goals in his first season in Swans colours and finished as the Championship's joint third top scorer with 22.

20 LIAM CULLEN

ATTACKER DOB: 23/04/1999 COUNTRY: WALES

The Kilgetty-youngster joined Swans at the age of 8 and worked his way through the ranks to make more than 30 senior appearances for the club.

He spent time on loan at Lincoln City during the 2021-22 season.

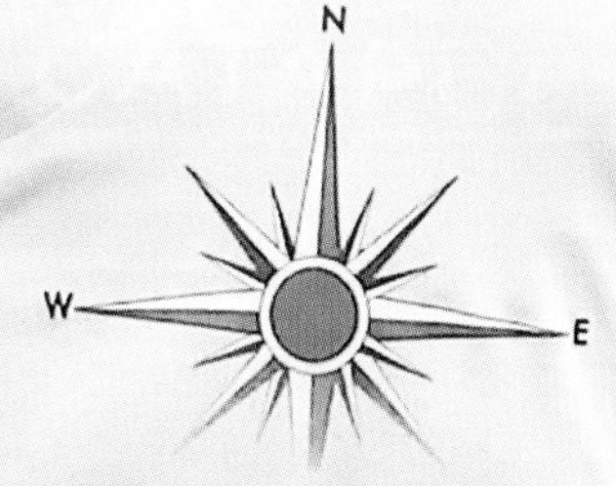

22 JOEL LATIBEAUDIERE

DEFENDER DOB: 06/01/2000 COUNTRY: ENGLAND

A product of the Manchester City youth academy, Joel Latibeaudiere arrived in SA1 in October 2020, signing a three-year deal.

Before joining the Swans, he spent the 2019-20 Eredivisie season on loan at FC Twente where he made five appearances and scored once.

23 NATHAN WOOD

DEFENDER DOB: 31/05/2002 COUNTRY: ENGLAND

Wood's arrival ahead of the 2022-23 season bolstered Swansea's defensive options. He is renowned for his composure in possession and athleticism, and also brings a physical presence.

An accomplished athlete - Wood was once ranked in the British top ten for his age group in the high jump - the defender joined the Middlesbrough academy set-up in 2015 and made his debut as a substitute in a 2018 Carabao Cup clash with Notts County.

CHAMPIONSHIP 2022-2023 SQUAD

26 KYLE NAUGHTON

DEFENDER DOB: 17/11/1988 COUNTRY: ENGLAND

The Sheffield United academy product joined Swans from Tottenham Hotspur in January 2015.

He is one of the club's longest-serving players and has wracked up more than 260 appearances in Swans colours. His cool head and calm demeanour is key to the way the Swans play.

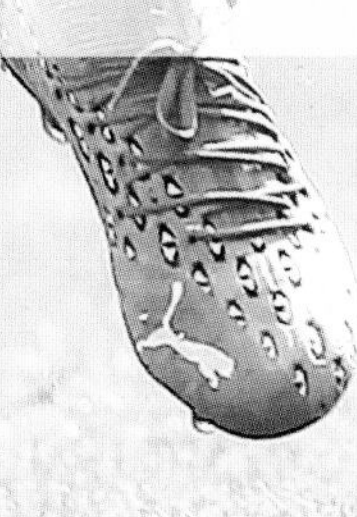

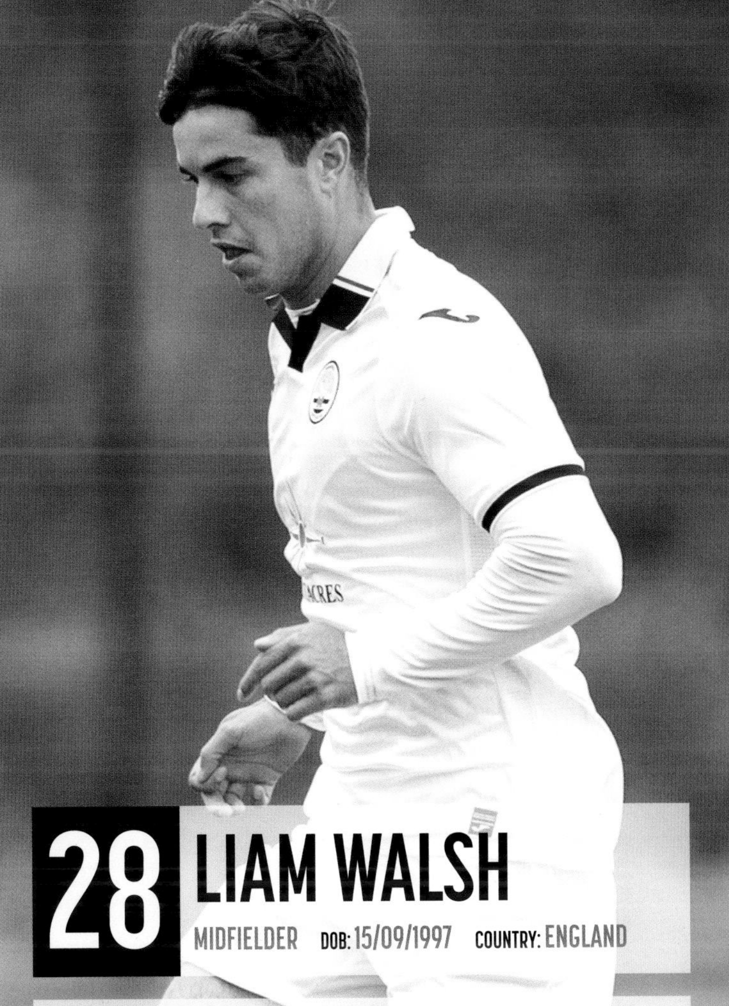

28 LIAM WALSH

MIDFIELDER DOB: 15/09/1997 COUNTRY: ENGLAND

Beginning his career with Everton, Walsh progressed through to the Toffees' under-23s, while he was loaned out to Yeovil Town and Birmingham City before signing for Bristol City on a permanent deal in 2018.

He made the switch to SA1 in July 2021. In his first season with the Swans he played a combined amount of seven matches in the Championship and cup competitions.

CHAMPIONSHIP 2022-2023 SQUAD

29 MATTY SORINOLA

DEFENDER DOB: 19/02/2001 COUNTRY: ENGLAND

The 21-year-old arrived in SA1 on a season-loan from Union SG. The player spent time in the youth ranks at Fulham before joining the MK academy in 2017, going on to sign a first professional deal in 2019.

Sorinola went on to enjoy a breakthrough campaign during the 2020-21 season, making 43 appearances in total as MK won plaudits for their attractive style of play.

31 OLLIE COOPER

MIDFIELDER DOB: 14/12/1999 COUNTRY: WALES

Ollie Cooper joined the Swansea City Academy at under-12 level. He broke into the first-team squad in 2020-21, making his debut in the FA Cup win at Stevenage.

He scored his first senior goal in the next round against Nottingham Forest, and went on to make three Championship appearances before the end of the season. He spent 2021-22 on loan at Newport County.

37 DAN WILLIAMS

MIDFIELDER DOB: 19/04/2001 COUNTRY: WALES

The central midfielder joined the Swans at under-eight level rising through the ranks and signing his first professional contract in the summer of 2019.

Williams made his senior debut in a 3-0 victory over Reading in the first round of the Carabao Cup in August 2021.

45 CAMERON CONGREVE

MIDFIELDER DOB: 24/01/2004 COUNTRY: WALES

Cameron Congreve joined Swansea City at pre-academy under-nine level and is a lifelong fan of the club.

The 18-year-old made his senior debut on 12 March against Blackpool. He subsequently made sub appearances against Cardiff City and Barnsley before making his first senior start away at Nottingham Forest in April.

He signed a first professional contract with the Swans in March 2022, and penned an improved extension a few months later in July.

MULTIPLE CHOICE

Here are ten Multiple Choice questions to challenge your footy knowledge!

Good luck...

ANSWERS ON PAGE 62

1. What was the name of Tottenham Hotspur's former ground?

A) White Rose Park
B) White Foot Way
C) White Hart Lane

2. Which club did Steven Gerrard leave to become Aston Villa manager?

A) Liverpool
B) Glasgow Rangers
C) LA Galaxy

3. Mohamed Salah and Son Heung-min were joint winners of the Premier League Golden Boot as the division's top scorers in 2021-22.

How many goals did they score?

A) 23 B) 24 C) 25

4. What is the nationality of Manchester United boss Erik ten Hag?

A) Swiss B) Dutch
C) Swedish

5. Where do Everton play their home games?

A) Goodison Road
B) Goodison Way
C) Goodison Park

6. From which club did Arsenal sign goalkeeper Aaron Ramsdale?

A) Sheffield United
B) Stoke City
C) AFC Bournemouth

7. What is Raheem Sterling's middle name?

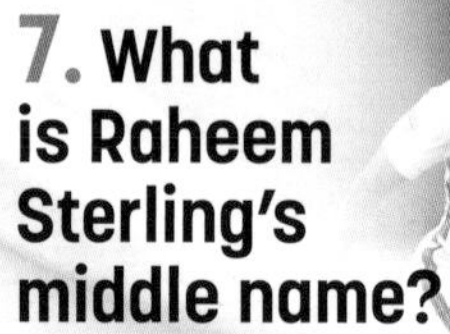

A) Shaun
B) Shaquille
C) Silver

8. Who won the 2021-22 League One Play-Off final?

A) Wigan Athletic
B) Sunderland
C) Rotherham United

9. How many times have the Swans won the League Cup?

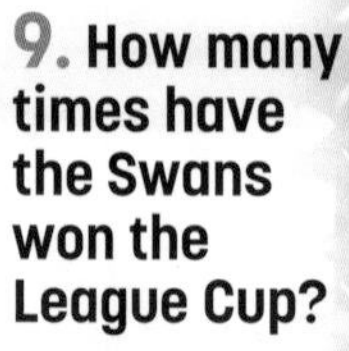

A) Once
B) Twice
C) Three times

10. Which Championship rival did 'keeper Ben Hamer join in July 2022?

A) Luton Town
B) Norwich City
C) Watford

5
BEN
CABANGO

ANSWERS ON PAGE 62

Cyril the Swan is hiding in the crowd in five different places as Swansea City fans cheers on the team at the start of the 2022-23 season. Can you find all five?

FAN'TASTIC

JOEL
PIROE
17

Close control in tight situations creates havoc in opposition defences - particularly when receiving the ball in the air - and nine times out of ten, when a striker receives the ball, he has his back to goal.

SOCCER SKILLS

RECEIVING THE BALL

Quite often the ball will arrive in the air, and good strikers have to be able to cope with that - controlling and turning in one movement, ready for the instant shot.

EXERCISE 1

In an area 20m x 10m, two players A and A2 test the man in the middle, B, by initially throwing the ball at him in the air, with the instruction to turn and play in to the end man - if possible using only two touches.

The middle player is changed regularly, and to make things more realistic, the end players progress to chipping the ball into the middle.

The middle player is asked to receive and turn using chest, thigh, or instep.

KEY FACTORS

1. **Assess flight early - get in position.**
2. **Cushion the ball.**
3. **Be half turned as you receive.**

EXERCISE 2

A progression of this exercise is the following, where the ball is chipped or driven in to the striker from varying positions. He has to receive with his back to goal, and using just two touches in total if possible, shoot past the keeper into the goal!

To make this even more difficult, a defender can be brought in eventually. For younger children, the 'servers' should throw the ball to ensure consistent quality.

Swansea University
Prifysgol Abertawe
joma
ATTACK

TRAIN TO WIN

Making sure that you are fit, healthy and fully prepared is key to success in whatever challenge you are taking on. Those three factors are certainly vital for professional footballers and also for any young aspiring player who plays for his or her school or local football team. The importance of fitness, health and preparation are key factors behind the work that goes into preparing the Swansea City players to perform at their maximum on matchday.

The Swans players will need to demonstrate peak levels of fitness if they want to feature in Russell Martin's team. Before anyone can think of pulling on a smart white shirt and stepping out at the Swansea.com Stadium, they will have had to perform well at the Training Ground to have shown the manager, his coaches and fitness staff that they are fully fit and ready for the physical challenges that await them on a matchday.

The players' fitness remains the all-important factor. Of course time spent practicing training drills and playing small-sided games will help a player's fitness but there is lots of work undertaken just to ensure maximum levels of fitness are reached.

Away from the training pitches the players will spend a great deal of time in the gymnasium partaking in their own personal work-outs. Bikes, treadmills and weights will all form part of helping the players reach and maintain a top level of fitness.

Over the course of a week the players will take part in many warm-up and aerobic sessions and even complete yoga and pilates classes to help with core strength and general fitness. The strength and conditioning coaches at the club work tirelessly to do all they can to make sure that the players you see in action are at their physical peak come kick-off.

While the manager and his staff will select the team and agree the tactics, analysts will provide the players and staff with details on the opposition's strengths, weaknesses and their likely approach to the match.

Suffice to say the training ground is a busy place and no stone is left unturned in preparation for the big match!

PLAYER OF THE YEAR

JOEL PIROE

Joel Piroe was named Swansea City Supporters' Player of the Season for the 2021-22 campaign at the club's annual awards dinner. The Dutchman enjoyed an outstanding first term in Swans colours, racking up 24 goals and six assists following his move from PSV Eindhoven.

His exploits saw him come out on top in our supporter vote via the club's website, while the 22-year-old also took home the top goalscorer prize. The forward was described by Russell Martin as a "beautiful footballer" when the head coach discussed the goalscorers technique and ability on a football pitch as well as "a brilliant person and a fantastic person".

Not only was Piroe effective in the No.9 role, he continued his impressive goalscoring form when he dropped deeper in order to accommodate Michael Obafemi. The pair struck up an impressive partnership in the latter part of the season with both scoring ten between January and May.

Having only managed seven goals in his two previous seasons combined, he initially set a target of ten and then 20. After beating his second target with six games to spare, he scored a further four goals to reach his final figure. Interestingly, his first brace for the club didn't come until 9 April scoring 18 goals in 18 separate games prior to that.

ACADEMY PLAYER OF THE YEAR

Cameron Congreve picked up the Academy Player of the Year award for the second year running after the 18-year-old had a breakthrough year in the senior team.

Making his debut as a late substitute in Swans away defeat at Blackpool in March, he went on to make another four appearances before the end of the season including starts against Nottingham Forest and Queens Park Rangers.

He put pen-to-paper on a new deal in the summer, and will be hoping to build on his progress last term as he sets his sights on regular first-team football for his boyhood club.

DREAM TEAM

Pick your ultimate Swansea City dream team and design them a kit!

SWANSEA
19
12
CITY A.F.C.

OLIVIER
10
NTCHAM

CHAMPIONSHIP DANGER MEN

24 STARS TO WATCH OUT FOR DURING 2022/23

BIRMINGHAM CITY

PRZEMYSLAW PLACHETA

A Polish international and true speed merchant, Przemyslaw Placheta is on a season long loan at St Andrew's from Championship rivals Norwich City.

The 24-year-old forward tends to operate on the left side of Blues' attack and marked his home debut for Birmingham City with a goal in their 2-1 victory over Huddersfield Town in August.

BLACKBURN ROVERS

LEWIS TRAVIS

All-action central midfielder Lewis Travis was at the heart of Blackburn Rovers' impressive 2021-22 Championship campaign featuring in all bar one of the club's league games last season.

With the ability to carry the ball forward and help his team turn defence into attack, 25-year-old Travis has won many admirers for his energetic displays in the Rovers engine room.

BRISTOL CITY

ANDREAS WEIMANN

Austrian international forward Andreas Weimann was the Robins' leading scorer last season with 22 goals in 45 Championship games.

An experienced and proven goalscorer at this level, Weimann, who had scored goals at second tier level for Watford, Derby County and Wolves before moving to Ashton Gate, netted in each of the first three league games of the new 2022-23 season.

BURNLEY

JAY RODRIGUEZ

Now in his second spell at Turf Moor, Burnley-born forward Jay Rodriguez is expected to have a big role to play for the Clarets in 2022-23 as the club looks to bounce back to the Premier League at the first attempt.

A former England international, Rodriguez played top-flight football for Southampton and WBA before rejoining the Clarets in 2019.

BLACKPOOL

THEO CORBEANU

Blackpool signed Canadian international forward Theo Corbeanu on a season-long loan from Wolves in July 2022.

Standing at 6ft 3ins, the 20-year-old brings a real presence to the Seasiders' attack and was on target in both of Blackpool's thrilling 3-3 draws against Burnley and Bristol City in August and following the sale of Josh Bowler he could well be the go-to man for goals at Bloomfield Road in 2022/23.

CARDIFF CITY

MAX WATTERS

Exciting striker Max Watters will be looking to cement his place in the Cardiff City attack in 2022-23. After joining the Bluebirds in January 2021 from Crawley, Watters was loaned to League One MK Dons in 2021-22.

However, Cardiff boss Steve Morison has handed Max the chance to make his mark with a series of starts as Cardiff's got the new season underway in impressive form.

COVENTRY CITY

CALLUM O'HARE

Attacking midfielder Callum O'Hare enjoyed a highly impressive 2021-22 season and has gained the reputation of being both City's star performer and one of the most creative midfielders operating in the Championship.

With fantastic close control and superb awareness of teammates, O'Hare is blessed with great balance when in possession and the eye for a decisive pass.

LUTON TOWN

ELIJAH ADEBAYO

Elijah Adebayo topped the Luton Town scoring charts last season with 16 Championship goals at the Hatters reached the end-of-season Play-Offs.

A strong target-man, Adebayo is expected to form an impressive strike partnership at Kenilworth Road this season with Luton new boy Carlton Morris who joined in the summer from Barnsley.

HUDDERSFIELD TOWN

JORDAN RHODES

Striker Jordan Rhodes has netted over 200 career goals since emerging though the Ipswich Town youth system back in 2007.

Now in his second spell with Huddersfield Town, 32-year-old Rhodes scored 87 goals in 148 outings during his first spell at the club. He returned to the Terriers in 2021 and scored the winning goal in last season's Play-Off semi-final against Luton Town.

MIDDLESBROUGH

MATT CROOKS

An all-action attacking midfielder who can also operate as an out-and-out striker, Matt Crooks joined Middlesbrough in the summer of 2021.

Signed on the back of a number of impressive seasons with Rotherham United, Crooks hit double figures in his first season at the Riverside and is sure to play a big part for Chris Wilder's team this time around.

HULL CITY

OSCAR ESTUPINAN

The Tigers completed the signing of Columbian international striker Oscar Estupinan in July 2022.

His arrival created a level of excitement around the MKM Stadium and the Columbian soon showed his capabilities with both goals as Hull pulled off a surprise victory over Norwich City in August 2022. A strong and mobile front man, Estupinan's goals may well help fire the Tigers up the table this season.

MILLWALL

BARTOSZ BIALKOWSKI

Polish international keeper Bartosz Bialkowski has been ever present in the Lions' last two Championship campaigns.

The 6ft 4in stopper is widely regarded as one of the most reliable goalkeepers in the division. Blessed with excellent reflexes, Bialkowski is an intimidating opponent in one-on-one situations and his command of the penalty area certainly provides great confidence for those operating in front of him

NORWICH CITY

TEEMU PUKKI

A Championship title winner on each occasion that he has played at this level, City's Finnish international striker will be searching a hat-trick of promotions from the second tier in 2022-23.

A real threat in and around the penalty area, Pukki netted 29 goals in the Canaries' 2018-19 title-winning campaign and 26 two season later as they went up as champions.

READING

THOMAS INCE

A much-travelled forward, Thomas Ince joined Reading on loan from Stoke City in January 2022 and played a key role him helping the Royals retain their Championship status last season.

Playing under the management of his father, Paul, Ince Jnr then joined Reading on a permanent basis in the summer of 2022. His attacking play and appetite to shoot from distance have won him great popularity with the Reading fans.

PRESTON NORTH END

EMIL RIIS JAKOBSEN

Former Denmark U21 international forward Emil Riis Jakobsen enjoyed a highly productive 2021-22 season with Preston North End.

A powerful 6ft 3in frontman, he was the side's standout performer with 20 goals in all competitions last season. The 24-year-old is blessed with great physical strength while also displaying calmness in front of goal.

ROTHERHAM UNITED

DAN BARLASER

Goalscoring midfielder Dan Barlaser weighed in with nine goals in Rotherham United's League One promotion-winning campaign.

He progressed through the Newcastle United Academy and after gaining valuable experience on loan with the Millers he joined on a permanent basis in October 2020. Seen as the man that makes United tick, a great deal will be expected of the 25-year-old former England youth international in 2022/23.

SHEFFIELD UNITED

OLIVER NORWOOD

Northern Ireland international midfielder Oliver Norwood is something of a Championship promotion-winning specialist.

The 31-year-old has previously won promotion from this division with Brighton, Fulham and as a Sheffield United player in 2018-19. He scored his first goal of the new season as the Blades defeated Blackburn Rovers 3-0 in the opening month of the season.

QUEENS PARK RANGERS

ILIAS CHAIR

The creative spark in the QPR team, Moroccan international Ilias Chair chipped in with nine Championship goals in 2021/22.

A true midfield playmaker, Chair has the ability to open up the tightest of defences and pick out teammates with his exquisite range of passing. The skilful Moroccan is sure to be the man that new Rangers boss Mike Beale looks to build his team around.

STOKE CITY

DWIGHT GAYLE

Much-travelled goal-getter Gayle joined Stoke City from Newcastle United in the summer of 2022.

A nimble front man with the ability to score all manner of goals, his arrival at Stoke was met with great delight. While on loan at WBA in 2018/19 he riffled home an impressive 23 Championship goals and the Potters with be hopeful of a good goal return from their new signing this season.

CHAMPIONSHIP DANGER MEN

24 STARS TO WATCH OUT FOR DURING 2022/23

WATFORD

KEINAN DAVIS

Following an impressive loan spell with Nottingham Forest last season, Aston Villa striker Keinan Davis will be keen to help the Hornets push for an instant return to the Premier League having agreed a season-long loan at Vicarage Road.

Standing at 6ft and 3ins, the 24-year-old striker has pace and power in abundance and is sure to thrill the Watford fans during his loan spell.

SUNDERLAND

ROSS STEWART

On target in SAFC's 2-0 League One Play-Off final victory over Wycombe Wanderers at Wembley, striker Stewart riffled home an impressive 26 goals in all competitions last season.

The Scotland international wasted little time in stepping up to the plate at Championship level as he netted two goals in his first three league games of the new 2022-23 season for the Black Cats.

WEST BROMWICH ALBION

KARLAN GRANT

Former Charlton Athletic and Huddersfield Town striker Karlan Grant scored 18 times in West Bromwich's Albion's 2021-22 Championship campaign.

The 25-year-old appears to be the go to man for goals again in 2022-23 for Steve Bruce's men and has already been on target in the Championship and EFL Cup this season.

SWANSEA CITY

MICHAEL OBAFEMI

A two-goal hero in Swansea City's 4-0 thrashing of South Wales rivals Cardiff City last season, pacy striker Michael Obafemi netted twelve Championship goals for the Swans last season.

Having formed a great understanding with fellow front man Joel Piroe in 2021-22, Swans' boss Russell Martin will have great hopes for Republic of Ireland international Obamfemi again in 2022-23.

WIGAN ATHLETIC

CALLUM LANG

A product of the Wigan Athletic academy, Liverpool-born forward Callum Lang has firmly established himself in the Latics' first team as an attacking player with the ability to create chances for teammates while also score goals himself.

The 23-year-old was in exceptional form throughout 2021-22 when he made 42 League One appearances and scored 15 as the Latics marched to the title.

MICHAEL OBAFEMI

9

TRUE OR FALSE?

Here are ten fun footy True or False teasers for you to tackle!

Good luck...

ANSWERS ON PAGE 62

1. England star Harry Kane has only ever played club football for Spurs

2. The FIFA World Cup in 2026 is due to be hosted in the USA, Mexico and Canada

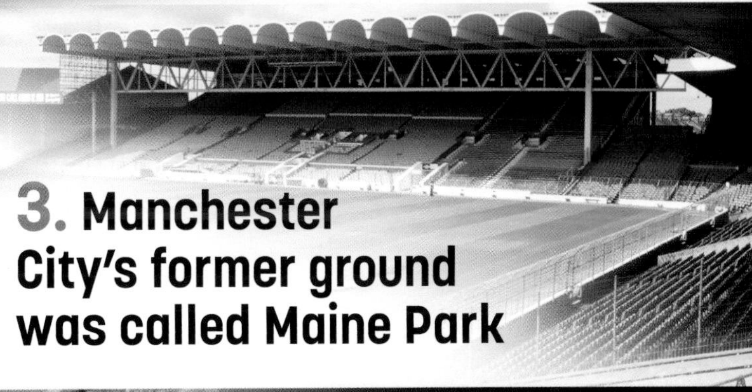

3. Manchester City's former ground was called Maine Park

4. Liverpool's Jurgen Klopp has never managed the German national team

5. Gareth Southgate succeeded Roy Hodgson as England manager

6. Manchester United's Old Trafford has the largest capacity in the Premier League

7. Jordan Pickford began his career at Everton

8. Huddersfield Town's nickname is the Terriers

9. Swans boss Russell Martin began his managerial career with Walsall

10. Joel Piroe netted 22 Championship goals for the Swans in 2021-22

NUMBER OF SEASONS WITH THE SWANS:

5

SWANS LEAGUE APPEARANCES:

166

SWANS LEAGUE GOALS:

83

PLAYER OF THE SEASON WINNER:

Never

LEGEND

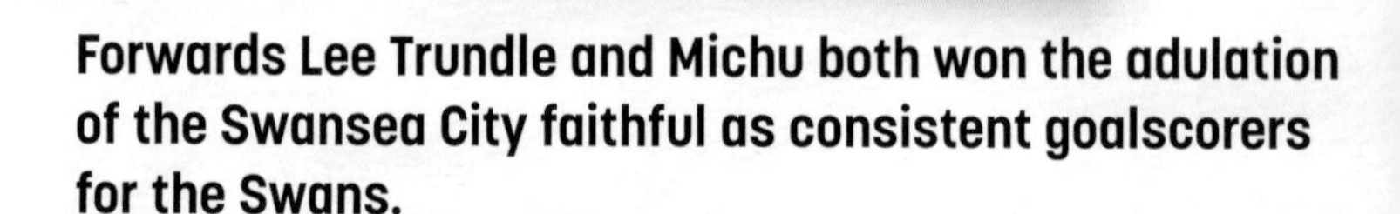

LEE TRUNDLE

SWANS ACHIEVEMENTS:

League Two promotion winners 2004/05

Football League Trophy winners 2005/06

MAJOR STRENGTH:

A flamboyant talent who was a threat to the opposition either in the air or on the deck

INTERNATIONAL ACTION:

Lee Trundle never played international football

FINEST HOUR:

Opening the scoring in the Swans' 2005/06 Football League Trophy final victory over Carlisle United

Forwards Lee Trundle and Michu both won the adulation of the Swansea City faithful as consistent goalscorers for the Swans.

Two skilful front men who led the Swans' attack and embraced the responsibility of being Swansea's go-to man for goals throughout their respective careers at the club. Both players possessed great physical presence and speed of thought which ensured that any central defender who was challenged with the task of marking them would certainly have known they'd been in a game.

Each player boasted an impressive goals-to-games ratio but who was the best? Well that's for you to decide and here are a selection of facts and figures from their time with the Swans to help you make your choice...

Once again, it's a tough call...!

NUMBER OF SEASONS WITH THE SWANS:

2

SWANS LEAGUE APPEARANCES:

52

SWANS LEAGUE GOALS:

20

PLAYER OF THE SEASON WINNER:

2012/13

LEGEND

MICHU

SWANS ACHIEVEMENTS:

League Cup winners
2012/13

MAJOR STRENGTH:

A great finisher with wonderful movement off the ball that helped him lead the attacking line

INTERNATIONAL ACTION:

Michu won his only international cap for Spain during his Swansea City career

FINEST HOUR:

Scoring the Swans' second goal in the 2013 League Cup final victory over Bradford City at Wembley

CLUB SEARCH

EVERY CHAMPIONSHIP TEAM IS HIDDEN IN THE GRID, EXCEPT FOR ONE... CAN YOU WORK OUT WHICH ONE?

J	B	R	A	L	G	V	N	O	R	W	I	C	H	C	I	T	Y	M	H
A	I	M	O	U	Z	E	K	F	X	R	W	F	U	C	C	D	I	S	W
B	R	I	S	T	O	L	C	I	T	Y	C	B	L	A	E	S	W	P	E
L	M	D	A	O	H	V	E	L	P	D	N	A	L	R	E	D	N	U	S
A	I	D	C	N	B	E	L	W	L	O	Q	I	C	D	W	Y	R	L	T
C	N	L	I	T	U	D	R	E	I	A	V	A	I	I	Q	P	D	O	B
K	G	E	T	O	U	N	U	H	P	U	W	H	T	F	I	T	E	L	R
B	H	S	E	W	H	E	B	N	A	I	O	L	Y	F	M	U	T	S	O
U	A	B	L	N	Y	H	T	V	R	M	J	N	L	C	H	D	I	C	M
R	M	R	H	U	O	T	K	L	N	C	U	S	G	I	J	J	N	Y	W
N	C	O	T	M	A	R	I	Y	O	W	T	N	D	T	M	Q	U	T	I
R	I	U	A	B	U	O	T	C	A	O	I	E	I	Y	U	R	D	I	C
O	T	G	N	U	F	N	S	T	A	D	P	G	M	T	M	X	L	C	H
V	Y	H	A	Y	S	N	F	C	A	E	I	K	A	S	E	M	E	E	A
E	I	G	G	E	G	O	I	E	K	O	S	B	C	S	Y	D	I	K	L
R	A	Q	I	L	R	T	R	P	L	U	E	N	O	A	O	E	F	O	B
S	H	T	W	D	Z	S	F	O	E	G	T	X	A	D	L	R	F	T	I
D	B	U	R	N	L	E	Y	R	A	S	O	A	K	W	I	B	E	S	O
C	O	V	E	N	T	R	Y	C	I	T	Y	R	F	N	S	B	H	Z	N
Q	U	E	E	N	S	P	A	R	K	R	A	N	G	E	R	S	S	A	H

Birmingham City
Blackburn Rovers
Blackpool
Bristol City
Burnley

Coventry City
Huddersfield Town
Hull City
Luton Town
Middlesbrough

Norwich City
Preston North End
Queens Park Rangers
Reading
Rotherham United

Stoke City
Sunderland
Swansea City
Watford
West Bromwich Albion

NATHAN WOOD

23

WHICH BALL?

Can you work out which is the actual match ball in these two action pics?

NAME THE SEASON

Can you recall the campaign when these magic moments occurred? Good luck...

ANSWERS ON PAGE 62

1. In which season did Chelsea last win the UEFA Champions League?

2. When were Manchester United last Premier League champions?

3. At the end of which season were England crowned World Cup winners?

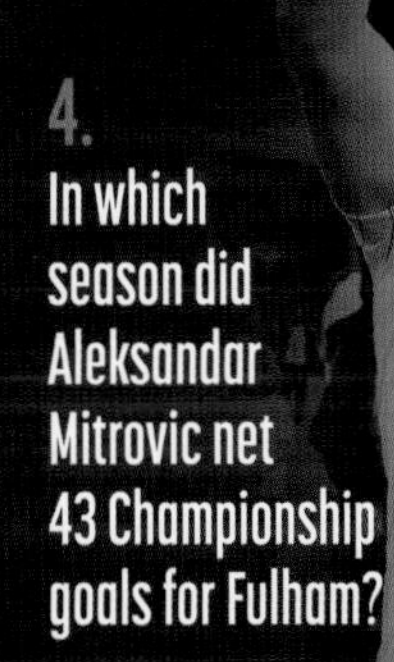

4. In which season did Aleksandar Mitrovic net 43 Championship goals for Fulham?

5. In which season did Leicester City become Premier League champions?

6. When did Tottenham Hotspur last reach the League Cup final?

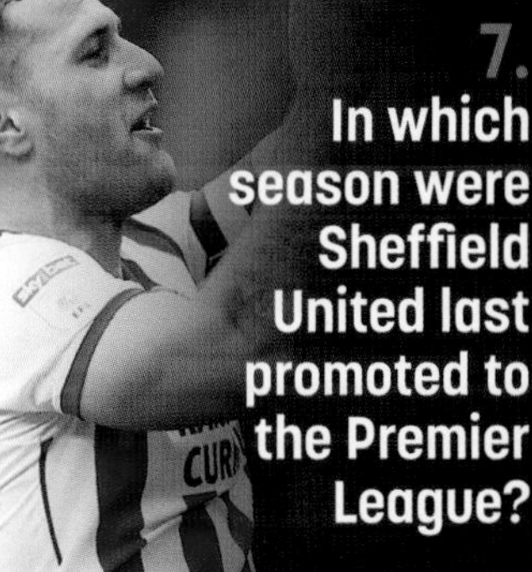

7. In which season were Sheffield United last promoted to the Premier League?

10. In which season did the Swans first register a South Wales derby league double over Cardiff City?

8. When did Manchester City win their first Premier League title?

9. During which season were the Swans last in the Premier League?

SWANS LADIES

Having claimed the league title for the previous two seasons, the odds were stacked against Swansea City Ladies with the introduction of a new league format and the addition of long-term absences for key players. But, come the end of the season, they were lifting the title for an impressive third time in a row.

The Swans had started their campaign earlier than their rivals as they turned in two commendable performances in the Champions League, including pushing professional side CSKA Moscow all the way to extra-time.

Swansea had been dominant champions in 2021, but this term was always likely to be more difficult, and so it proved.

They suffered their first league defeat in more than three years and, despite registering an unprecedented 17-0 win over Coed Duon Women in the first round, the Ladies bowed out at the quarter-final stage of the Welsh Cup, losing out on penalties to Cardiff Met and missing out on the chance to complete the double.

Despite additional challenges, the side showed resilience, determination, and professionalism to overcome hurdles and take the league title. In 2022-23, they are looking to continue their formidable form, progress further in the cup and retain the title for a fourth season.

Swansea University
Prifysgol
Abertawe
macron
DEW XG

ANSWERS ON PAGE 62

WHO ARE YA?

Can you figure out who each of these Swans stars is?

HARRY
DARLING
6
WESTACRES

TRUE COLOURS

Can you colour in this picture of Harry Darling?

FAST FORWARD>>

Do your predictions for 2022/23 match our own?...

PREMIER LEAGUE CHAMPIONS

Liverpool

CHAMPIONSHIP WINNERS

Swansea City

CHAMPIONSHIP

CHAMPIONSHIP RUNNERS-UP

Norwich City

PREMIER LEAGUE

PREMIER LEAGUE RUNNERS-UP

Chelsea

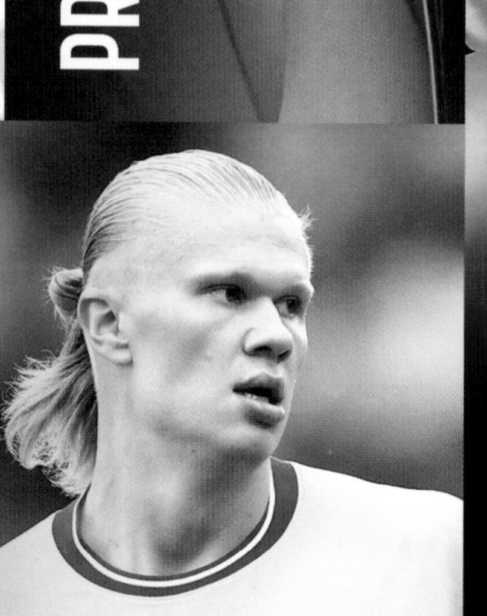

PREMIER LEAGUE TOP SCORER

Erling Haaland

CHAMPIONSHIP TOP SCORER

Michael Obafemi

LEAGUE ONE TOP SCORER

Conor Chaplin

FA CUP WINNERS

Spurs

LEAGUE CUP WINNERS

Leicester City

LEAGUE ONE CHAMPIONS

Derby County

CHAMPIONS LEAGUE WINNERS

Real Madrid

LEAGUE ONE RUNNERS-UP

Oxford United

EUROPA LEAGUE WINNERS

Roma

NUMBER OF SEASONS WITH THE SWANS:

14

SWANS LEAGUE APPEARANCES:

566

SWANS LEAGUE GOALS:

3

PLAYER OF THE SEASON WINNER:

Never

LEGEND

ROGER FREESTONE

SWANS ACHIEVEMENTS:

Football League Trophy winners 1993-94

Football League Third Division winners 1999-2000

MAJOR STRENGTH:

A big penalty-box presence who was lways happy to take command of his area

INTERNATIONAL ACTION:

s a Swansea player, Roger was capped once by Wales in a match against Brazil in 2000

FINEST HOUR:

In 1995 Freestone briefly became the club's designated penalty-taker and successfully converted three out of three spot-kicks for the Swans

Swansea City Football Club has a long and proud history of fielding excellent goalkeepers and both Roger Freestone and Michel Vorm were two fine stoppers who starred between the posts for the Swans.

As the last line of defence, both Freestone and Vorm produced a host of match-winning saves throughout their spells in South Wales while marshalling the defensive unit in front of them. While Freestone was an integral part of the team that began the club's rise through the divisions, Vorm featured in the exciting Premier League era. But who was the best? It's a tricky one to decide and here are a number of facts and figures from their time with Swansea City to help you reach your decision...

Yet again, it's certainly a tough call...!

LEGEND

MICHEL VORM

NUMBER OF SEASONS WITH THE SWANS:

3

SWANS LEAGUE APPEARANCES:

89

SWANS LEAGUE GOALS:

0

PLAYER OF THE SEASON WINNER:

2012/13

SWANS ACHIEVEMENTS:

Football League Cup winners 2012-13

MAJOR STRENGTH:

An athletic 'keeper with great reflexes and superb anticipation of danger

INTERNATIONAL ACTION:

A full international with the Netherlands, Michel continued to win caps for his country while playing for the Swans

FINEST HOUR:

In August 2011, Vorm saved a penalty form Wigan's Ben Watson to give the Swans their first-ever Premier League point

IDENTIFY THE STAR

Can you put a name to the football stars in these ten teasers?

Good luck...

ANSWERS ON PAGE 62

1. Manchester City's title-winning 'keeper Ederson shared the 2021-22 Golden Glove award for the number of clean sheets with which Premier League rival?

2. Which Portuguese superstar re-joined Manchester United in the 2021-22 season?

3. Can you name the Brazilian forward who joined Aston Villa in May 2022 following a loan spell at Villa Park?

4. Who became Arsenal manager in 2019?

5. Who scored the winning goal in the 2021-22 UEFA Champions League final?

6. After 550 games for West Ham United, which long-serving midfielder announced his retirement in 2022?

7. Who took the mantle of scoring Brentford's first Premier League goal?

8. Who scored the final goal for Manchester City in their 2021-22 Premier League title-winning season?

9. Which former Swansea City star returned to the club in the summer of 2022 following spells with Liverpool and Stoke City?

10. Can you name the Swansea player who joined the club from Exeter City in January 2015?

KYLE
NAUGHTON
26

ANSWERS

PAGE 26 · MULTIPLE CHOICE

1. C. 2. B. 3. A. 4. B. 5. C. 6. A. 7. B. 8. B. 9. A. 10. C.

PAGE 28 · FAN'TASTIC

PAGE 43 · TRUE OR FALSE?

1. False, Harry played on loan for Leyton Orient, Millwall, Norwich City & Leicester City. 2. True. 3. False, it was called Maine Road. 4. True. 5. False, Gareth succeeded Sam Allardyce. 6. True. 7. False, Jordan began his career at Sunderland. 8. True. 9. False, he began his managerial career with MK Dons. 10. True.

PAGE 46 · CLUB SEARCH

Huddersfield Town

PAGE 48 · WHICH BALL?

PAGE 49 · NAME THE SEASON

1. 2020/21. 2. 2012/13. 3. 1965/66. 4. 2021/22. 5. 2015/16. 6. 2020/21. 7. 2018/19. 8. 2011/12. 9. 2017/18. 10. 2021/22.

PAGE 52 · WHO ARE YER?

1. Michael Obafemi. 2. Kyle Naughton. 3. Matty Sorinola. 4. Ryan Manning. 5. Jamie Paterson. 6.Nathan Wood. 7. Harry Darling. 8. Joel Piroe.

PAGE 60 · IDENTIFY THE STAR

1. Allison Becker (Liverpool). 2. Cristiano Ronaldo. 3. Philippe Coutinho. 4. Mikel Arteta. 5. Vinícius Júnior. 6. Mark Noble. 7. Sergi Canós. 8. İlkay Gündoğan. 9. Joe Allen. 10. Matt Grimes.